# Koby the
# Koala

by Jan Latta

Reading consultant: Susan Nations, M.Ed., author/literacy coach/consultant in literacy development

Science and curriculum consultant: Debra Voege, M.A., science and math curriculum resource teacher

GARETH**STEVENS**
PUBLISHING
A Member of the WRC Media Family of Companies

Hello. My name is Koby, and I am a koala. I live in Australia, where my **ancestors** have lived for over 15 million years.

Some people think koalas are bears. That is not true!
We are **marsupials**. Like kangaroos or opossums, we
have pouches to carry our babies in.

Meet Kim, my baby sister. She is ten months old.

Our mom will look after Kim until she is about one year old. Then Kim will go live on her own. When Kim is about two, she will start her own family. For now, she enjoys riding on Mom's back. It is great fun!

My dad is almost twice as big as my mom. He weighs about 26 pounds (12 kilograms). He has a dark scent **gland** on his chest. He uses the gland to mark his **territory** with his smell. He also lets others know where he is by tilting back his head and making a loud noise. It sounds like a cross between a bullfrog's croak and a gorilla's roar. It also sounds like a snorting burp!

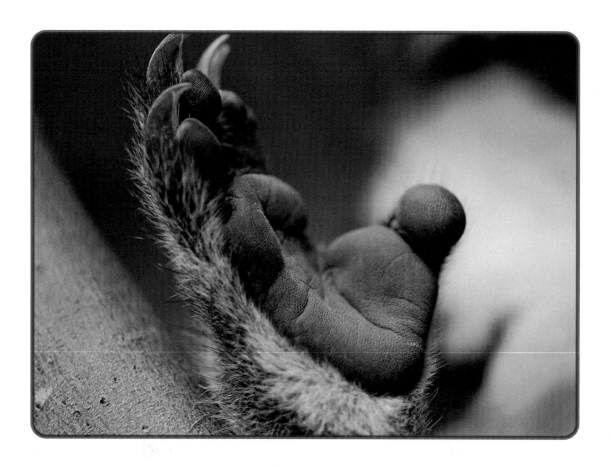

I have very powerful feet. My strong, sharp claws help me climb trees and hold onto branches.

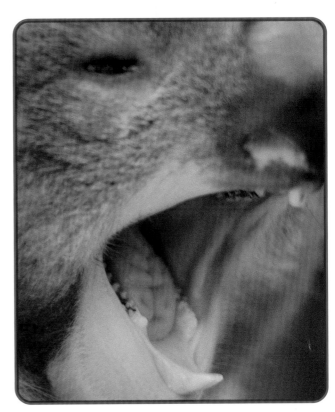

I have a large black nose and sharp front teeth. My eyes are shaped like almonds. My fluffy ears are big.

My home is in the **eucalyptus** trees. They give me shade and comfortable branches to rest on. Most important, they give me leaves to eat. Without these trees, I would not **survive**.

Koalas are **herbivores**, which means we eat plants. We are fussy eaters. Even though there are hundreds of kinds of eucalyptus trees, we eat the leaves and buds of only a few.

Sometimes we feed on other trees, such as coast tea trees and golden wattle and cherry trees.

Koalas spend up to twenty hours each day sleeping and resting. We sleep a lot to save energy. Eucalyptus leaves are thick and tough, so it takes lots of energy to **digest** them.

We do other things besides sleep. We climb a lot, and we **groom** ourselves.

And look!  We can jump from tree to tree.

We can walk on the ground, too. I must watch out for dogs and cars, which can hurt me. I move slowly when I am on the ground. If something dangerous comes, however, I can run fast and climb into a tree to get away.

Koalas can live in the wild for about twelve years, but every year there are fewer of us. People cut down more eucalyptus trees, destroying our **habitat**.

Some people have come up with ways to help us keep living in the wild. They are protecting our trees and planting more of them. We need enough eucalyptus trees for our whole wild family.

# Koala Facts

**Did You Know?**

• A koala's fingerprints do not match any other koala's fingerprints.

• Koalas need to be around many types of eucalyptus trees so they can eat a variety of leaves.

• The koala's stomach is special. Even though eucalyptus leaves are poisonous, koalas do not get sick from them.

• Koalas get most of their water from the leaves that they eat.

• Koalas get their name from an Aboriginal word that means "no drink." The Aborigines were the first people to live in Australia.

• When it is cold, koalas curl up into a ball to keep warm. When it is hot, koalas stretch out on tree branches to catch the breeze and cool off.

• Koalas are more active at night than during the day.

• When it is born, a baby koala is about the size of a jelly bean.

• Koalas can live up to twenty-one years in zoos and protected areas.

• Australia is the only place where koalas can live in the wild. They live on islands along the coast and in the woods on the mainland.

• People used to hunt koalas for their fur. In the 1920s, they killed so many koalas that some parts of Australia did not have any koalas.

• People continue to destroy the koala's habitat.

• Foxes, pet dogs, and wild dogs called dingoes also hunt koalas.

• There used to be millions of koalas in Australia. Today, there are as few as 300,000.

# Map — Where Koalas Live

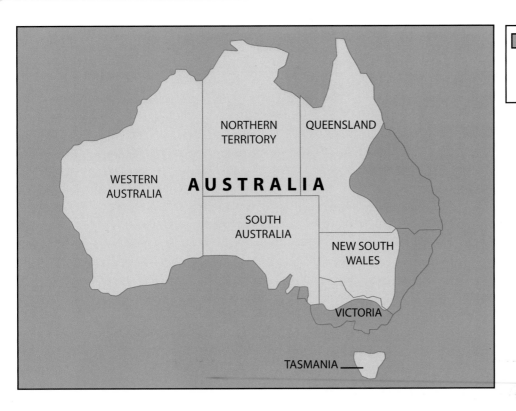

— Koalas live in the dark green area of the map.

# Glossary

**ancestors** — relatives that lived long before one's parents were born

**digest** — to break down food in the stomach

**eucalyptus** — a type of evergreen tree with tough, thick leaves

**gland** — a small opening in the skin that produces liquid

**groom** — to lick, brush, and clean

**habitat** — the environment, or place, where an animal lives

**herbivores** — animals that eat only plants

**marsupials** — mammals that have a pouch to carry their young

**survive** — to live

**territory** — the area where an animal lives and which it claims as its own

# More Information

## Books

*Baby Koala*. Nature Babies (series). Aubrey Lang (Fitzhenry & Whiteside Limited)

*Koala*. Welcome Books (series). Edana Eckart (Children's Press)

*Koalas and Other Marsupials*. What Kind of Animal Is It? (series). Bobbie Kalman and Robin Johnson (Crabtree Publishing Company)

## Web Sites

Australian Marsupial Mammals
*education.qut.edu.au/~masters/EC_projects/Abeya/assignment.htm*
Chrissy Koala and her friends tell you about their family and relatives.

National Geographic Kids: Koalas
*www.nationalgeographic.com/kids/creature_feature/0008/koalas.html*
Send a post card, find fun facts about koalas, watch a video, and more.

**Publisher's note to educators and parents:** Our editors have carefully reviewed these Web sites to ensure that they are suitable for children. Many Web sites change frequently, however, and we cannot guarantee that a site's future contents will continue to meet our high standards of quality and educational value. Be advised that children should be closely supervised whenever they access the Internet.

Please visit our Web site at: **www.garethstevens.com**
**For a free color catalog describing Gareth Stevens Publishing's list of high-quality books and multimedia programs, call 1-800-542-2595 (USA) or 1-800-387-3178 (Canada). Gareth Stevens Publishing's fax: (414) 332-3567.**

**Library of Congress Cataloging-in-Publication Data**

Latta, Jan.
    Koby the koala / by Jan Latta. — North American ed.
        p. cm. — (Wild animal families)
    Includes bibliographical references.
    ISBN-13: 978-0-8368-7769-4 (lib. bdg.)
    ISBN-13: 978-0-8368-7776-2 (softcover)
    1. Koala—Juvenile literature. I. Title.
QL737.M384L38    2007
599.2'5—dc22                        2006032126

This North American edition first published in 2007 by
**Gareth Stevens Publishing**
A Member of the WRC Media Family of Companies
330 West Olive Street, Suite 100
Milwaukee, WI 53212 USA

This U.S. edition copyright © 2007 by Gareth Stevens, Inc.
Original edition and photographs copyright © 2005 by Jan Latta.
First produced as *Adventures with Kolah the Koala* by
TRUE TO LIFE BOOKS, 12b Gibson Street, Bronte, NSW 2024 Australia

Acknowledgements: The author thanks Jon Resnick and George Apostolidis, who generously allowed reproduction of their photographs.

Project editor: Jan Latta
Design: Jan Latta

Gareth Stevens editorial direction: Valerie J. Weber
Gareth Stevens editor: Tea Benduhn
Gareth Stevens art direction: Tammy West
Gareth Stevens Graphic designer: Scott Krall
Gareth Stevens production: Jessica Yanke and Robert Kraus

Printed in Canada

1 2 3 4 5 6 7 8 9 10 10 09 08 07 06